T0146833

The Colors
of *Life*

The Colors of Life

JEFFREY M. RUSSO

THE COLORS OF LIFE

iUniverse books may be ordered through booksellers or by contacting:

iUniverse
1663 Liberty Drive
Bloomington, IN 47403
www.iuniverse.com
1-800-Authors (1-800-288-4677)

ISBN: 978-1-5320-0171-0 (sc)
ISBN: 978-1-5320-0170-3 (e)

Library of Congress Control Number: 2016910798

Print information available on the last page.

iUniverse rev. date: 08/03/2016

To my parents, Angelo and Lorraine. I couldn't have asked for better. Thank you both for raising me to be the man I have become.

To my best friend, Todd. Thanks for always being able to make me laugh.

To Stephen DiGiovanni and Albert Audette, two of the kindest men I've ever met. I thank you both for encouraging me in my writing.

To Leslie, your friendship means a great deal to me, for you were the one who brought the magic back again so I could write.

To Christina, I can't thank you enough for what your presence brought to my life. You'll forever hold a place in my heart.

My Two Muses

Most artists have a muse
to inspire their creative fire.
But I've been more than fortunate,
for I have been graced with two.
The first is the woman of my dreams
who I once loved completely,
an integral part of my soul.
She was the focus of my very first poem.

Fate intervened with the second woman, and she's become
a cherished friend indeed. Without even trying, she has
influenced me to begin writing anew, after years of inactivity.

Both are spirited beauties who unexpectedly entered my life at
difficult times, lifting me from the despair I was in, helping me
to see the colors of life and always to find a new story to write.

The Slightest of Seconds

Have you ever wondered what could occur in the slightest of seconds?

You just might look into the eyes of a woman
who will influence your life
in ways you never deemed possible,
a woman who pulls you from hopeless despair,
unbosoms your pain,
helps you to laugh once again,
encourages you toward your dreams—
a woman who you'll fall in love
with every second that you can.

My Favorite Pen

My favorite pen
is nearing its end
as letters fade away
across the page.
The inkwell inside
will soon run dry.

My favorite pen
rolls naturally in my hand,
helping me scribe all the
words that fill my mind
and simply scratch away the mistakes.

My favorite pen
feels like an old friend
sharing a story with the other.
Now I must reluctantly
break in another and
grow to cherish it
along the pages.

His Wooden Drumsticks

The musician spun his
wooden drumstick atop his palms
with practiced precision—
then wailed upon his drums
with an intense musical rhythm.

The percussion instruments
roared like a rumble of thunder
pulsing through the air
as he brought the forceful tones
to lively fruition.

His hands beat down with
quickening speed,
entertaining the exuberant crowd
with an explosive
resonance of sounds.

To Stand in Line

Remember when we were young
and had the time to stand in line
to purchase tickets for a movie premiere
we'd been eagerly waiting to see.

Hours passed surprisingly fast
as the line grew steadily longer.
We talked and laughed with friends
and other fellow fans
about our screen hero's adventures,
biding our time
until the box office window opened.

The Artist's Rendering

The artist's rendering
of a friend's young daughter,
who wore a white-dotted blue dress
with a pretty flower
attached at her waist,
was incredibly precious.
The brushstrokes
and colors chosen captured
the lovely girl's essence.

Her soft yellow hair
was drawn back
from her smiling face
by a tiny blue ribbon
that perfectly matched
the cute dress she was wearing.

A Strong Chemistry

In a dalliance that shouldn't be,
there's a strong chemistry
that exists between us
whenever our eyes meet.

I know you can feel
the strength of its pull
just the same as I.

Please don't fight it
with indifference.
Instead, let nature take its course,
emerge, and liven,
only to see
where it might lead us.

Her Ebony Dark Eyes

Her ebony dark eyes
are an alluring sight
that complements her light brown skin
and winning smile.

So deep and stark of color
when looked into,
they appear as if
black pools of water.

A pleasing darkness
only enriches
her intrinsic glow,
making her a striking beauty
to behold.

Happy Birthday

The flaming candles
atop your cake
express that
upon this date
an exceptional person
was born.

So before you make a wish
or tear open your presents,
know in your heart
that your family and friends
cherish your presence,
for love you convey
to all without pause.

The First Flower of Spring

From under the hard-packed dirt
and decomposing leaves
wriggles free
the first flower of spring
with its fledgling young stem
and glorious yellow bulbs,
readying themselves to burst open
to the beckoning rays of sun.

Freshly Cut Grass

Spring has arrived.
The temperature is rising nicely outside
as the flowers
bloom with life.

I sit atop the steps
of the old stone porch,
feeling the warmth
of the morning sun,
watching
as my neighbor begins
to mow his lawn.

The freshly cut grass
is a sweet delight
as I savor
the natural aroma
that spreads throughout the sky.

The Ancient Barn

The dawning morning sun
peeks just above
the ancient wooden barn
that has stood along the shore
of Cove Island
since the early 1900s.

Beams of bright light
stream across the darkened rooftop
to reflect upon
the calm water,
cutting through the lingering shadows
while a bevy of pearly white swans
glide peacefully about.

The Rumbling Roar

I heard the rumbling roar
of motorcycles right outside
my front door.

Possibly Harleys,
but I'm unsure,
for they had passed
by the time I reached
the bay window—
a beckoning call
to fellow enthusiasts
that riding season
is nearly here.

Wild Crocuses

The steep grass hill
was filled with a covering of rich colors
as the wild crocuses
flared open
from the invigorating sun,
looking like lovely little jewels,
certain to enhance the view.

A Relaxing Summer Day

It's a splendid summer day
as I lie in
the refreshing shade
of a broad dogwood tree.

I watch a bumblebee
with fascination
as it delicately
pollinates the bountiful flowers around me.

A pleasant breeze
sweeps below the leaves,
relaxing my tired body
enough to fall asleep.

A Golden Butterfly

A golden butterfly
flew effortlessly
about the powder-blue sky
with a flutter
of its decorative soft wings.

It swirled around the maple trees
then down toward the ground,
gliding whimsically
above the vibrantly white daisies.

The Full Moon

As the full moon hung low
in the charcoal sky
it shimmered magnificently
through the silky clouds of night,
providing a shadowy roadway
below with light.

The Perfect Healing Balm

The walk along the well-
worn trails
of the nature museum
is peacefully serene.

As the sun peeks through
the shade of the tall trees,
the running stream crackles
against the rocks
along the bank.

Small frogs spring
from the muddy leaves,
while insects sing in unison,
hidden in their surroundings.

The tranquil walk
through nature's calm
is a respite from our troubles,
the perfect healing balm.

Clamming with Family

My uncle, my father, and I
wade into the low tide
in search of clams
to indulge upon
with our families.

With our bare feet,
we step and feel
for the smooth shells
embedded in the dense sand.

Once they are found,
we dive beneath the dark waters
to retrieve them
with our hands
and place them in quantity
in our net sacks.

The Hunter

The hunter stalks his prey
with delicate steps,
trying not to disturb the earth
or startle the beast he seeks.

He follows his quarry's tracks
and the tufts of fur
snagged on twigs.

Finally locating his prize,
he raises his rifle
level with his eye
and squeezes the trigger.

A Tumbleweed

A friend set off on a journey out west,
but before he left,
he asked if I wanted a souvenir upon his return.
I replied in jest that I wanted a tumbleweed.

Several weeks had passed
since my friend departed,
and I'd all but forgotten
when a midsized package
arrived for me by mail
with no return address.
I was surprised
to see that the content
was a pristine tumbleweed.

A Beautiful Desert Cactus

The beautiful desert cactus
flourishes in the blistering heat
with its thick, spiny green stem
and bold red flowers.

The hardy plant is miraculous
as it survives and even thrives
against the absence of moisture
in the arid desert sand.

Impeccable Loveliness

She emerged from the pool with an enticing smile
and a profoundly beautiful face,
with her dark brown hair
hanging in wet tendrils down her back.

She carried her ample physique proudly,
and the pink bikini she wore
fit perfectly
as she graced all that lounged around
with a view of impeccable loveliness.

Utter Silence

As I ready myself for bed,
I draw open the window
to listen to
the soothing sound of night—
only to hear nothing
but utter silence outside—
no cars driving along the street
or cicadas chirping from the trees,
no feral cry of animals
or even the slightest breeze to ruffle the leaves
on this unusually quiet night.

A Summer Moment

The pure blue sky was limitless
with nary a roaming cloud in sight,
and the sun's glare
was unbearably harsh to the eye
as I heard the summer birds
warble a song
from the bordering trees
and watched the abundant leaves
flit in the wayward breeze.

A Relatively Young Tree Stands Dead

A relatively young tree stands dead
amid the tranquil beauty of a well-kept street.
Not a single rich leaf garnishes its branches.

The colorless trunk is a rueful sight,
as the bark has fallen along the grass.

Its lifespan cut short by nature's whim,
it is waiting only to fall
either in a strong storm or a man's sharp saw.

The Sound of the Cicada

The humidity is stifling and heat oppressive
as the sun withers the landscape
and simmers the streets.

Only a hot breeze blows,
and it's difficult to breathe
as I hear the shrill screeching
of the cicadas
clinging to the abounding trees.

A Cooling Noon Rain

A cooling noon rain
finally came
near the end of the searing hot week.
Pouring down from the ominous-looking clouds,
it pelted against the hot asphalt street
and rose as a light, white steam.

The Sun-Ripened Pears

By the side of an active road,
a cluster of sun-ripened pears had grown to fruition
upon a vast green tree,
clinging ever so firmly
across its limbs.

Fortunately, a low-hanging branch
was just within hand's reach.
You plucked down one of the sweet fruits
and drew it toward your mouth to eat.

The Playground

The playground is alive with delighted children
as the chain-link swings sway back and forth.

Giggling rings out from the youngsters
who grow dizzy from spinning
on the merry-go-round.

Others glide quickly down the polished slide,
almost believing they could fly,
adding a smile to their tiny faces.

Fireworks

The floating barge's mortars
rumble to life,
firing an array of fireworks
into the calm black sky.

They explode with a rainbow of colors
that illuminates the night
and they echo for what seems like forever
on this Fourth of July.

The Exhilarating Experience

My girlfriend and I
stepped onto the amusement park ride
that was designed
to look like a flying saucer.

Once we were inside the circular compartment,
there were vertical handles
to hold onto,
but neither belts nor bars
to hold us immobile.

The attraction was based
on centrifugal force,
for it would be impossible
to move as it spun sideways.

The chamber blurred in the speed
as we curved a full ninety degrees.

When the ride finished,
we were quite light-headed
but thrilled
by the exhilarating experience.

A Pure Delight to Witness

On my way to dinner,
I saw a beautiful woman across the busy street
as she slowed my stride to a halt
on this late-August afternoon.

She wore a figure-hugging,
light white dress
that complemented her sculpted, sexy body.
As she strolled with purse in hand,
her sand-brown hair
blew back from her shoulders
in the tender breeze.

She entered through the large glass doors
of a luxury apartment building—
and was gone.
But seeing her for those fading few seconds
was a pure delight.

The Forceful Sight of Nature

From out of the slate sky,
a raging tempest roared,
wailing down upon a massive oak tree
that stood impervious
against the storm.

Dark green leaves
were torn violently from the tree
and flung about the streets,
as the weaker limbs cracked
and crumbled
with a rush of wind.

The strong gale thrashed endlessly at the tree,
and the force of nature
was truly astounding to see.

Sawing through a Broken Dead Branch

In the humid summer heat,
I saw through a broken dead branch
dangling from a tall tree
as beads of warm sweat
roll down over me.

Wood shavings irritate my eyes
as my arms begin to ache,
but I continue to saw,
cutting a notch across the damaged limb
until I hear it crack.
I watch it fall to the ground
under its own weight.

The Late-Summer Morning

The late-summer morning grows cooler
as the leaves sense that fall subtly approaches
and begins to transform color.

A sizable spiderweb twinkles
in the dawn light
as it extends between two lawn chairs sitting outside.

A solitary leaf falls
tumbling across the spiderweb
and lands softly atop the lawn chair,
where it lies idly in the sun.

A Redheaded Woodpecker

I hear a drumming rap from above,
and I seek to find where the reverberating clamor is coming from,
only to see a redheaded woodpecker
striking away at the hallowed tree,
chipping apart a small opening
with its chiseled beak
to form a new nest for sleep.

The Summer Is Over

The summer is over.
Kids have returned to school,
and the lush morning grass
holds the slightest hints of dew.

A few colored leaves
have fallen from the trees,
and the late-blooming flowers
are being descended upon
by a hoard of eager bees.

The summer is over.
Fall is drawing closer.
And the squirrels begin their search for acorns
with a scurrying pace.

The Seagull by the Sea

A sole white seagull
rests passively by the sea,
perched atop a massive boulder
that stands along the blackened shore
as a coastal storm steadily approaches.

Strong waves crash
against the enormous stone,
and harsh a wind blows
only to ruffle
the untroubled bird's feathers.

A Brilliant Bushel of Pink

As I head out for the day,
there's a hurricane raging
hundreds of miles away
that still overshadows this Saturday
with a chill sky of gray.

I veer around a bend in the road
and am astounded to see
a brilliant bushel of pink flowers
gleaming in the cold
as a sprinkle of rain falls,
and the raw wind bites at me.

Grown Calm

The morning air is sweet
and the sky a splendid sapphire,
as the day-breaking sun
peeks between the fleeting clouds.

After a tumultuous night
of terrifying winds
that easily toppled thick trees,
blocking numerous streets,
it has finally grown calm.

A Sorrowful Sight

It was a sorrowful sight
to see amid the loose debris
a delicate red robin
lying dead by the side of the street.

There was no apparent harm
that befell its sleek, feathery body,
so I wondered to myself
what might have caused
its unfortunate demise.

The Super Moon Lunar Eclipse

On the crisp September night,
the neighborhood motioned outside,
standing on their sidewalks,
patios, and driveways to witness
the super moon eclipse.

The camaraderie was welcoming,
as people gathered
with hardy laughter and excitement
to share
this rare celestial event.

As the night grew late,
cameras flashed
and recorders rolled
while the moon
slowly turned red.

The Sleek Colored Streets

After the rain had fallen,
the sleek colored streets
glimmered with the various hues of the city:
a glaring stream of white from the legion of cars' headlights,
a fluorescent shine from the theater's bright neon lights,
a steady glow of yellow from the street lights,
and the intense beams of either red or green
from the overhanging traffic lights,
decorating the damp pavement
with a shimmering band of colors
to stir the eye's sensation.

Sea Foam

As the morning tide rolls in,
sparkling from the sun,
a frothy stripe of white sea foam
rounds the boundary
of the rock-covered shore.

A thick tuft of yellow-green sea grass
juts out of the water
and sways rhythmically
in the cool coastal breeze.

An Exquisite Red Maple Tree

I rode along a secluded street.
Autumn foliage drifted in the breeze
as I sat atop my bicycle seat,
rolling beneath an exquisite red maple tree
that still held on to its dark vibrancy.

I raised my hand from the handlebar
and glided my fingers whimsically across the soft leaves
while admiring their impressive crimson shading.

A Surprising October Snow

An unlikely heavy, wet snow fell from the
surprisingly cold October sky,
coating all the vibrant autumn leaves white.

The ground was dressed
not with fall foliage
but with winter splendor.
Some of the trees, still holding their leaves,
were overburdened with the fracturing weight.
Squealing limbs snapped violently
from the strain.

The Sleeping Black Cat

The very end of the sleeping black cat's tail
still wagged tenderly
while its soothing purr rang out.
The cat had curled into a soft little ball of fur
atop its favorite blanket.

It's Halloween Night

It's Halloween night.
All has fallen dark,
and the pumpkins are carved
with scary expressions.

The porch light is on,
and the bowl filled with candy is ready
while I wait for the first knock.

I see all the children
dressed in their fun-filled costumes
as they scream,
"Trick or treat!"

A Majestic Autumn Dance

A subtle chilly breeze
grazed across a lovely tree,
unsettling a reddish-orange leaf from its twig.
The leaf spiraled down colorfully toward the lawn
in a majestic autumn dance.

A Charming Fall Melody

I can hear the tune of the autumn leaves
as they play a charming fall melody
as they tumble down from the various trees
then skitter across the rooftops in the breeze
or crackle along the streets.

I can hear the rustling sound
when people traipse through the small mounds
with the gentle stride of their feet.

Thanksgiving Morning

It's Thanksgiving morning,
and I indulge in my holiday tradition
of watching the classic Laurel and Hardy film
March of the Wooden Soldiers.
I hear a tremendous roar rise from the stadium nearby;
a football player must have scored.

The dining room is festively dressed,
and the aroma of turkey spreads throughout the house.
I ready the yams for baking
and cut the freshly made bread into thin slices
to share soon with the family I cherish.

An Enormous Hawk

I saw an enormous hawk
settled on a hibernating tree
with its head slouched low,
showing no movement at all
as the wind whipped the tips of its brown-feathered wings.

All of a sudden
a baby bird cried out from another tree,
awakening the hawk.
I watched its dark head rise with its hooked razor-sharp beak.
Its eyes darted around momentarily,
and then it fell back to sleep.

The First Freeze of the Season

By late afternoon, the shining sun falls and dusk sets in
as a forceful winter wind blows, carrying a bitter cold
that rattles the signs on the street
and brushes across the resting trees,
bringing along the first freeze of the season.

A Snowflake at Midnight

A solitary snowflake
fell from the darkened heavens
at midnight,
fluttering through the frosty air
with a reflective shine
underneath the incandescent moonlight—
then tenderly touched the earth
below a beaming lamplight.

The Sound of Footsteps

Click clack, click clock.
I hear the echoing knock of a woman's footsteps
on this late-winter evening
as her heels clap down against the icy pavement.

She walks toward her warm, welcoming home
with a quick pace,
scurrying from the cold to reach her front door.
Her footsteps slowly grow silent in the distance.

The Red Cinnamon Candle

The red cinnamon candle
encased within a glass vase
burns with a meager flame
atop the mantelpiece.

The charred wick melts into the soft wax,
emitting a spicy scent that permeates the den.

Its flickering light creates a shadowy glow
that dances upon the darkened ceiling at night.

Two Silver Pigeons

A cold rain tore down
on a gloomy winter night
as two silver pigeons
with bold white stripes across their tail feathers huddled,
their wings together,
by the corner of an old stone windowsill.
They were trying to keep warm
during the bitter, wet storm.

To Enthrall My Eyes' View

On an early winter's eve
I see beyond a span of trees
that daylight plummets
quickly to night,
shading the heavens
with an astounding red hue
that looks as if the sky were aflame
to enthrall my eyes' view.

With Romantic Cheer

Our minds were filled with a charming, memorable sight
as we stepped out of the theater doors
on a chill wintery night.

We delighted to see a swirling flurry of
snowflakes fall from the overcast sky.

It livened the season with romantic cheer,
as it dressed the bustling city with a sparkling cover of white.

A Naturally Beautiful Woman

It's a mid-December morning.
I'm standing at the end of a long line at the store
with several holiday items in hand
and I lay eyes on a naturally beautiful
woman poised behind the register.

I finally reach the counter and slide my items forward.
I am captivated by her twinkling smile as
she greets me with a chipper hello.
Her long black hair rolls over the royal-blue blouse she wears.

We engage in idle conversation for a moment,
and her personality sparkles as much as her lovely appearance,
and I noticed there is not a smidge of makeup
on her delicate olive skin,
which only enhanced her pretty face.

Holiday Lights

The street is dressed gleefully with holiday lights
that line the trees and bushes with an assortment of showy colors
that glow iridescently with a blink or twinkle
that pleases the sight along the row of homes
that illuminate the cold winter night.

A Warm Christmas Day

It's December 25th,
but it hardly seems like Christmas because it's so warm outside.
Even though the horizon is shaded winter
gray and the large trees now sleep,
the lawn still grows and is green as can be.

But inside, the walls of the home tell a festive story,
as carols play joyfully on the radio and the colored lights glisten
on the beautifully dressed tree.
Wrapped presents yet to be opened rest beneath its branches
on this warm Christmas Day.

New Year's Eve

The touch of cold air doesn't faze the jubilant crowds
that stand in Times Square,
as the clock ticks closer to the start of the new year.

The spirited affair is televised everywhere:
a remarkable crystal sphere hovers midair,
ready to descend once the countdown commences
to consummate the unforgettable celebration.

The Blizzard

Waves of heavy snow wallop the city endlessly
as the overlay of white continues to rise.

The numbing winds wail down from the dismal sky,
and the piercing flakes bite at your skin.

As the blowing snow whips about the air,
it covers the foot trails rapidly
while visibility declines,
and everything finally
grinds to a halt.

Why? Why? Why?

I wake from the sound of the morning alarm
and ready myself for work in the dark,
only to see through the window that it obviously snowed overnight;
everything is dressed in silvery white.

I open the doors slightly only to be slapped by the cold.
As I look up with tired eyes to see a drab morning sky,
I think,
Why? why? why? must I venture outside?

Ten Degrees

The sun is as luminous as I've ever seen,
but that doesn't change the thermometer from reading only
ten degrees.

My mornings begin outdoors.
Even though I'm dressed in heavy clothes,
the arctic freeze causes my eyes to water and sends shivers
right down to my knees.

The Icy Shoreline of Holly Pond

The shade-covered shoreline of Holly Pond
was quite a sight to see, as the inflowing tide
slowly froze due to the exceptionally frigid temperatures overnight.
It formed an aesthetically pleasing icy sheet.

Tiers of rippling waves were beautifully frozen in place,
encircling the rocks and reeds protruding from the seabed.
They will surely melt away with the upcoming day's gleaming sunrise.

The Windowpane

The windowpane shudders in the wailing winter wind
as it sits loosely inside the worn wooden frame.

The unwavering strong gusts lash against the window,
creating a light jangle
that fills the old house
with a tranquil night song.

As the Winter Nears Its End

In the waning days of February,
I saw a white patch of snow
clinging to a dark shingled roof.

I watched it swiftly melt away in the growing strength of the sun.

It streamed down into the metallic drain
spout with a light trickling sound
as winter neared its end.

A Most Precious Little Girl

She was a precious little girl no taller than my knee,
with adorable blue eyes and tiny blonde pigtails.
Still learning to walk,
she wobbled unsteadily on her feet,
possibly because of the jacket she wore that was nearly as long as she.
Her mother kept a watchful eye from only a few steps away.

The Last Mound of Snow

Although the sun grew warmer by the day,
the last remaining mound of snow refused to let go.

Being covered in filth and litter hinders its thaw,
as it begrudgingly dissolves into its original form.

Writer's Block

When you don't feel like you have anything left to write,
the brain has grown silent,
nothing rhymes anymore,
no fresh ideas merge words together,
you can't start that all important first line,
so you place your pen down,
for that's when a new story will finally flow from your mind.

Insomnia

Sleep. Why can't I fall asleep?
For it's been longer than a week, and I need to get some sleep.

All I do is toss against the bed and turn beneath the sheets.

So I rise every night and slowly pace the creaky wooden floors,
seeking a remedy to end my restlessness.

I hope that my eyes will finally close
for at least one evening
of blissful sleep.

The Early-Morning Express Train

The railway warning arm lowered
as the train rolled into the station.
A crowd of weary travelers boarded the
railcars and rested in the seats.

The conductor blared the horn
and released the brakes from the heavy steel wheels.
The train lurched forward
and rumbled over the wrought iron rails
as it headed toward a dawning New York City.

Growing Friends

Besides some photographs I've viewed, I have yet to see you,
nor have I heard the sound of your voice.

I immensely enjoy the conversations we share
across the miles through social media.

You're friendly and kind,
and you enthusiastically answer the simple
questions that rise in my mind.

Whether through chance or fate,
friends we're becoming, and I wouldn't have it any other way.

Leslie

A pretty woman I know,
who I've only seen in a photo,
helps to relieve my troubles
as she shoulders hers alone.

I admire her strength.
While I grow weak with doubt, she suffers
with worry but laughs it aside.

The Lord only knows how important she's become to me.
I hope she feels the same.
From the moment we first chatted, a friendship was made
that I truly hope lasts for the rest of our days.

That Smile

That smile of hers is brighter than I've ever witnessed
as it gleams from her pristine face.

That smile of hers is a calming force with the
ability to lessen a turbulent night.

That smile of hers is a joy to behold and enlivens
a gathering just by her attendance.

That smile of her is comely and sweet,
and when you first get a glimpse of it,
you want the chance to meet her.

Her BeguilingBrown Eyes

Her beguiling brown eyes were undoubtedly pretty,
as were her features,
being blessed with a flawless complexion,
shapely nose, and deep-pink lips.

She had her fair blonde hair pulled to the left
side of her face when I first saw her.

But her eyes held a hint of sorrow that I hope,
whatever her plight may be,
time will someday mend.

A Favorite Song

When you hear the opening melody and
know it's from your favorite song,
a smile broadens across your face.
Then the lyrics bring you back
to a special time or place.

The volume is raised as your hands start to clap
and your feet begin to tap
along with the booming music.

Singing out loud with every note is rollicking fun,
making us feel
once again
young.

A Game of Pool

Twist your cue into the blue chalk,
take aim at the billiard rack,
and strike it apart
with an explosive crack.

The colored balls scatter around the felt-covered table
with a rattling clatter
as you visualize the shot
you're about to make.

The cue stick glides effortlessly between your forefinger and thumb
as you draw your arm back,
stroking each ball
with driving force
toward the designated pockets.

I Met a Celebrity

When I saw a celebrity whose work I respected,
I hesitated,
for the fan in me wanted to rush over and meet him,
but the man in me wanted to leave him to his privacy.

I pondered each choice for a few moments,
and the fan won out.
So I slowly approached with my hand held out,
telling him that I appreciated his past works
and wishing him continued success.

He smiled politely and thanked me,
then shook my outstretched hand, which enamored me greatly
as we both turned
and went our separate ways.

It's Time for Peace

"IT'S TIME FOR PEACE"
was written in graffiti along the wall of the expressway bridge
in bold colored letters.

I'll never know who the person was that crafted those markings.
And as the world becomes more violent,
I believe he or she is right.

Unbeknownst Gifts

This wondrous world we live upon
shares a bounty of gifts with us,
which we're usually in too much of a hurry to realize:
hearing the joy of a child's laughter or the
sweet scent of lilacs in bloom,
finishing the last scoop of an ice cream sundae
or watching the lion roar at the zoo.
These cause a smile to grow upon our faces
because we never consciously thought we genuinely needed them.

Well after Midnight

It's well after midnight
when a poem comes to mind
that I need to jot down on a blank sheet of paper
before I forget.

It's well after midnight,
and time grows late.
I have to wake for work in the morning,
but completing this poem
is just as important.

It's well after midnight,
and still I write.
A sound sleep is what I need
as my eyes feel weary,
so I put aside my pen,
for now my writings are finished.

Her Flaming Red Hair

Her flaming red hair
is wonderfully exquisite
in all the imaginative ways
that she fashions it.

It's commonplace to see her,
and every time I do, her hair is different.
Whether ironed straight, blown wavy, or
any other of many variations,
her flaming red hair
is a visual sensation.

I Wish I Could Be There

I wish I could be there for you
to share some of my strength with you
or bestow a comforting hug
that I believe you need
or buy a book for you to read
or even a soft scarf to keep you warm.

You already have my moral support,
my respect and even my love,
but these are only my words.
Hopefully they'll be enough.

A Relaxing Evening at Home

It's Friday night,
the work week is over,
dinner is finished,
and the plates have been cleaned.
Time for a relaxing evening at home.

I'm tired and sore,
so I lie across the carpeted floor
with a warm afghan covering me,
and I fall asleep shortly after I turn on the TV.

My View from the High-Rise

My view from the high-rise window was astounding
as I looked down upon the beauty and activity of the city
and the contrasting architecture—older buildings and new—
and the weathered crosses atop the church steeples.

The remarkable bridges that span the rivers,
and the colorfully rolling vehicles, and
even the legion of people milling about the streets
were truly fascinating to see.

Has the Distance Taken Its Toll?

Is there something I've done to offend you—
some betrayal of trust or an unkind slight?

For your silence slices me deeper than a knife.
I don't believe I've hurt you.

Has the distance taken its toll,
damaging what was once a strong bond
that I hope someday we'll be able to reclaim?

I feel badly that you might have chosen to walk away.
My love for you is
and always
will be true.

Forever

You stepped into my life at a very dark time,
captivating my heart
and changing my life for the better.
I'll always love you
forever.

Sadly the same doesn't hold true for you.
There's nothing I can say or do,
but I know deep inside
that you hold a special place in your heart for me too.
I'll take that with me till my very last day.

An old, cherished friend I wish to become
so that we can still share some laughter in the sun—
maybe a time or two more,
filled with a lot of fun,
that we can keep in our thoughts
for all the years to come.

The Rail Yard

It's early morning
and still very dark outside
when I hear in the distance
a loud wail coming from the rail yard
as the conductors warm the engines
for the impending day's travels.

Two Good Men

I'm more than likely on the final job of my career
as I've worked for municipalities, large churches, and
small businesses over the years. I've grown older
and a little slower,
but I feel like I still have something more to give.

I was once told that as a man ages it's more
difficult to form new friendships.
I'm not sure if that's true,
for I work with two good men:
Rafal and Ben.
And I am honored to call them terrific friends.

Though both are younger than I,
we share similar traits and laugh together every day.
They are both supremely adept at their skill sets,
and they teach this aging man some new capabilities.

A Former Teacher

Grocery store Sundays are usually mundane,
but this week wasn't entirely the same.

As I turned past the isle, I came across a great
former teacher shopping with his wife.

I recognized him immediately,
though he'd aged considerably and had a white beard.
Overwhelmed by fondness, I approached him to reintroduce myself
and to talk for a moment.
He no longer remembered me, and that's all right,
for how many countless students had he met during his life.

I shook his hand,
thanking him for the devotion and guidance he provided
in helping me to become a respectable person.

Old Friends

Old friends are a comfort to see,
for you can picture both past and present in the same view.

You hear of times past that can still make you laugh
or watch their grown children readying for college or marriage.

Old friends who still remain in town may have
grown portly or even a little gray,
but good memories never fade.

As one sidled up beside me just the other day,
while I was ordering pizza,
we looked at each other with amusement
for all that had come before.

Bedtime

It's late, and the house has grown silent
except for the ticktock of the clock
as I ready myself for bed.

I hear my elderly mother's gentle snore from behind her bedroom door
as she sleeps warm beneath her sheets.
I hope she's dreaming of pleasant things.

My Loving Mother

My loving mother is slowly losing her battle with Alzheimer's,
but it seems that the maternal instinct never falters.

Once, when I arrived home from work, aching and with a fever,
I told her that I couldn't care for her that evening.

So she, instead, tried her best to take care of me,
covering me with a blanket
and placing a cool facecloth on my forehead
until I fell asleep.

I Stay

I'm in a responsibility-laden cage,
and the only key to unlock the door is love.
It's the only reason I stay.

I'm lonely.
God, I am so lonely
and scared that my own life
is ever so slowly slipping away.

I stay because I believe it's right.
I stay for my ill mother,
who gave me life.
But I am exhausted by the strain.
God, please watch over me,
and keep me safe.

Eulogy

My beloved father,
my beloved friend,
I've never known a more honorable, gentle man,
and I'm struggling to cope with the fact
that our time has come to an end.

I know that you're already in heaven,
watching over me,
and I pray that I live as honorably
as I can, with the hope
that someday
I'll get to be with you again.

Printed in the United States
By Bookmasters